Name

_____

Surname

_____

Address

_____

_____

Phone

_____

Mobile

_____

E-mail

_____

PERLA COLLECTION

ISBN 978-1-911424-94-9
SKU/ID 9781911424949

Cover design by Fabio Perla
"DESIRE OF YOU"
Sanguigna pencil on wood cm60 x 60 - Year 2013

Book design by Wolf Graham
Editor: Wolf Graham

Publishing Company:
Black Wolf Edition & Publishing Ltd.
Scotland
www.blackwolfedition.com

PERLA COLLECTION

[signature]

ISBN 978-1-911424-94-9
SKU/ID 9781911424949

Cover design by Fabio Perla
"DESIRE OF YOU"
Sanguigna pencil on wood cm60 x 60 · Year 2013

Book design by Wolf Graham
Editor: Wolf Graham

Publishing Company:
Black Wolf Edition & Publishing Ltd.
Scotland
www.blackwolfedition.com

www.ingramcontent.com/pod-product-compliance
Lightning Source LLC
Chambersburg PA
CBHW021127080526
44587CB00012B/1171